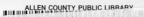

WILLIAMS
Bryan

FULTON
Wauseon
Napoleon

Toledo LUCAS

OTTAWA
Port Clinton
Sandusky

Painesville
LAKE
Chardon
GEAUGA

Jefferson
ASHTABULA

DEFIANCE
Defiance

HENRY

Bowling
Green
WOOD

SANDUSKY
Fremont

ERIE

Cleveland
CUYAHOGA

Elyria
LORAIN

TRUMBULL
Warren

Paulding
PAULDING

PUTNAM
Ottawa

Findlay
HANCOCK

SENECA
Tiffin

HURON

Norwalk

Medina
MEDINA
Akron

SUMMIT
Akron

PORTAGE
Ravenna

Youngstown
MAHONING

Van Wert
VAN WERT

ALLEN
Lima

WYANDOT
Upper
Sandusky

CRAWFORD
Bucyrus

RICHLAND

Ashland
ASHLAND
Mansfield

WAYNE
Wooster

STARK
Canton

Lisbon
COLUMBIANA

Celina
MERCER

AUGLAIZE
Wapakoneta

HARDIN
Kenton

Marion
MARION

Mt Gilead
MORROW

HOLMES
Millersburg

New
Philadelphia
TUSCARAWAS

Carrollton
CARROLL

SHELBY
Sidney

LOGAN
Bellefontaine

UNION

Delaware
DELAWARE

KNOX
Mt Vernon

COSHOCTON
Coshocton

HARRISON
Cadiz

JEFFERSON
Steubenville

DARKE
Greenville

CHAMPAIGN
Urbana

MIAMI
Troy

Marysville

COLUMBUS

FRANKLIN

LICKING
Newark

GUERNSEY
Cambridge

St Clairsville
BELMONT

Eaton
PREBLE

MONTGOMERY
Dayton

Springfield
CLARK

London
MADISON

MUSKINGUM
Zanesville

NOBLE
Caldwell

Woodsfield
MONROE

GREENE
Xenia

PICKAWAY
Circleville

FAIRFIELD
Lancaster

PERRY
New
Lexington

McConnelsville
MORGAN

WASHINGTON
Marietta

BUTLER
Hamilton

Lebanon
WARREN

Wilmington
CLINTON

FAYETTE
Washington CH

HOCKING
Logan

HAMILTON
Cincinnati
Batavia

CLERMONT

Hillsboro
HIGHLAND

ROSS
Chillicothe

McArthur
VINTON

ATHENS
Athens

BROWN
Georgetown

ADAMS
West Union

Waverly
PIKE

Jackson
JACKSON

MEIGS
Pomeroy

SCIOTO
Portsmouth

GALLIA
Gallipolis

LAWRENCE
Ironton

The New

Enchantment of America

OHIO

By Allan Carpenter

CHILDRENS PRESS, CHICAGO

ACKNOWLEDGMENTS

For assistance in the preparation of the revised edition, the author thanks:
PHILIP DEVORE, Director, and MARIAN A. PAOLIELLO, Publications Editor, Office of Travel and Tourism, Department of Economic and Community Development, State of Ohio, and EDWARD R. ENTZ, Chief Audio-Visual Specialist, Ohio Historical Society/Historical Center.

American Airlines—Anne Vitaliano, Director of Public Relations; *Capitol Historical Society*, Washington, D.C.; *Newberry Library,* Chicago, Dr. Lawrence Towner, Director; *Northwestern University Library*, Evanston, Illinois; *United Airlines*—John P. Grember, Manager of Special Promotions; Joseph P. Hopkins, Manager, News Bureau.

UNITED STATES GOVERNMENT AGENCIES: *Department of Agriculture*—Robert Hailstock, Jr., Photography Division, Office of Communication; Donald C. Schuhart, Information Division, Soil Conservation Service. *Army*—Doran Topolosky, Public Affairs Office, Chief of Engineers, Corps of Engineers. *Department of Interior*—Louis Churchville, Director of Communications; EROS Space Program—Phillis Wiepking, Community Affairs; Charles Withington, Geologist; Mrs. Ruth Herbert, Information Specialist; Bureau of Reclamation; National Park Service—Fred Bell and the individual sites; Fish and Wildlife Service—Bob Hines, Public Affairs Office. *Library of Congress*—Dr. Alan Fern, Director of the Department of Research; Sara Wallace, Director of Publications; Dr. Walter W. Ristow, Chief, Geography and Map Division; Herbert Sandborn, Exhibits Officer. *National Archives*—Dr. James B. Rhoads, Archivist of the United States; Albert Meisel, Assistant Archivist for Educational Programs; David Eggenberger, Publications Director; Bill Leary, Still Picture Reference; James Moore, Audio-Visual Archives. *United States Postal Service*—Herb Harris, Stamps Division.

For assistance in the preparation of the first edition, the author thanks:
Consultant Margaret Hatch, Director, Education Department, Ohio Historical Society; Mabel Morsbach, Cincinnati Public Schools; Koder M. Collison, Director, Department of Industrial and Economic Development for Ohio; Glenn A. Rich, Director, Division of Elementary and Secondary Education, Ohio Department of Education; and Anthony Wayne Parkway Board and Education Service of the Ohio State Museum.

Illustrations on the preceding pages:
Cover photograph: Cincinnati, American Airlines Photo
Page 1: Commemorative stamps of historic interest
Pages 2-3: Riverfront Stadium, American Airlines Photo
Page 3: (Map) USDI Geological Survey
Pages 4-5: Cincinnati Area, EROS Space Photo, USDI Geological Survey, EROS Data Center

Project Editor, Revised Edition:
 Joan Downing
Assistant Editor, Revised Edition:
 Mary Reidy

Library of Congress Cataloging in Publication Data

Carpenter, John Allan, 1917-
 Ohio.
 (His The new enchantment of America)
 Includes index.
 SUMMARY: Discusses the history, natural resources, places of interest, and famous citizens of the Buckeye state.
 1. Ohio—Juvenile literature.
[1. Ohio] I. Title. II. Series.
F491.3.C3 1978 977.1 78-16162
ISBN 0-516-04135-5

Contents

The present official state seal of Ohio shows the rising sun very much as Worthington and his friends must have seen it.

A True Story to Set the Scene

A SEAL IN THE SUNRISE

All night long a group of men had been working at a very hard task. As they discussed the many difficulties in their way, they began to wonder if they ever would solve the problem that faced them.

This was an important matter, for if they made the right decisions, the great territory of Ohio would become a state. Many people wanted statehood for Ohio, but many were strongly against it. The foes of statehood included the governor of the territory himself, Governor Arthur St. Clair. He knew his influence would come to an end as soon as Ohio became a state.

When Thomas Worthington called the meeting, this was the problem he and his friends faced and tried to solve at Worthington's estate called Adena. To this handsome, new home came the leaders of the group calling for statehood, under the leadership of Worthington and his brother-in-law, Dr. Edward Tiffin.

At last Mr. Worthington and his friends felt they had found a plan which was bound to lead Ohio to statehood. They closed their meeting and went out on the terrace of the beautiful estate.

At that moment, the sun came up behind the mountains in the distance. It was a scene none of the men would ever forget. They felt that here was a new dawn for the territory they loved so much.

But this was a scene which residents of Ohio will never forget for an entirely different reason. They see it everywhere almost daily.

Worthington and his friends were so impressed they decided that scene would become the official state seal. And so it did!

There have been many changes in the seal over the years, but today every textbook on Ohio, every reference book and, of course, every official Ohio document carries the scene of a bright sun rising over Worthington's field, with a shock of grain in the right foreground and a sheaf of arrows representing the seventeen states of the Union, including Ohio.

Probably no other state seal ever had a similar history, but this is just one of the many stories of the enchantment of Ohio.

Ohio's development owes much to its many waters, such as Put-in-Bay.

Lay of the Land

"It will be our own fault if we are not the happiest people in the Union," said the first Ohio historian about his state. He meant that Ohio had everything needed to make people happy—soil, climate, natural resources, and location.

When the earliest explorers pushed across the Allegheny Mountains in the East, they found that after the difficulty of getting through the mountains Ohio was like a great gate, opening up the whole West. Ever since, Ohio has been called the "Gateway State."

One "gate" on the north is Lake Erie. The other "gate," the Ohio River, glides for 450 miles (724 kilometers) along the southern and part of the eastern boundary. These great bodies of water have formed natural boundaries for Ohio from the time the first men came into the region.

Because of their importance, we might call the rivers the lifelines of Ohio. In addition to the Ohio River itself, other important rivers are the Muskingum, Mahoning, Hocking, Scioto, Miami, Little Miami, Grand Chagrin, Cuyahoga, Black, Vermilion, Huron, Sandusky, Portage, and Maumee.

Some of these rivers flow into the Ohio River, while others empty into Lake Erie. This means that there is an Ohio "divide" just as there is a continental divide.

In addition to the rivers, Ohio has about 500 lakes. Most of these are artificial rather than natural bodies of water, but this makes little difference to the people who use and enjoy them.

Another "body of water" that has been very important to Ohio has never been seen by man. It is hard to imagine today that Ohio was ever covered by an ocean, but the land was on the bottom of the sea, not once but many times. Each time the land rose above the sea, plants grew and animals appeared. Then once more the land sank; the seas came in, and everything was covered with the slime of the ocean bottom. In this way the deposits of minerals—coal, oil, gas— found in Ohio today—were built up under the pressure of all the gathering layers of materials over millions of years—possibly 60,000,000 years in all.

Right: Millwood is a fine place to study Ohio's geography. Below: Grooves were carved by Nature in Kelley's Island State Park.

The next great natural event in Ohio came many millions of years later, when for some unknown reason the climate became much colder, and great sheets of ice from Canada forced their way across much of the state, carrying everything in their path.

For thousands of years, Ohio was in a deep freeze. Then the climate grew warmer and the ice slowly melted. This happened four times altogether. Wherever the ice had been, the great force of pressure of its weight and power had changed the surface completely; it leveled the hills and filled in the valleys, leaving a thick layer of rich soil.

A large area across the southern and eastern part of the state never was covered by glaciers, and it still has an entirely different appearance from the part where the glaciers came.

Near Hillsboro is Serpent Mound. Shaped like a snake, the mound has seven curves. The state carefully preserves this well-known mound.

Footsteps on the Land

VANISHING RACES AND DISAPPEARING INDIANS

The earliest people in Ohio roamed the land hunting game for food. We have only the most uncertain means of knowing they ever existed, but occasionally a chipped flint has been found with the skeleton of an animal we think lived about the same time as these early people. They left no pottery or other indications that they had the skills for making such things.

Much later, probably about six or seven thousand years ago, another group of people made their home in Ohio. We call them the Archaic people. There are definite traces that these people really did exist, but we know very little about them.

Still another group of people lived in Ohio, about the time of Christ, possibly 2,000 years ago. These are called the Adena people.

At Adena, the estate of Thomas Worthington, workers in 1901 were restoring the estate as a part of a new museum. They were digging when they uncovered a log building used as a tomb by these ancient people. In the tomb were their skeletons, weapons, and ornaments.

Now archeologists call the whole group the Adena people, because of this first discovery at Adena.

Most famous of all the prehistoric people of Ohio are the Hopewell Indians. The small hills, or mounds, that they left were first found on the farm of a man named Hopewell, in Ross County.

The sculpture, pottery, and other art work found in these mounds indicate that the Hopewell people had a rather advanced civilization. Some of the mounds are very large and complicated in shape, such as the effigy mounds in the form of eagles, snakes, or other figures.

Such mounds could only have been made by people who knew about construction. Many objects found in Hopewell mounds prove that they must have traded with faraway lands, such as Mexico.

One of the largest Hopewell centers in Ohio, called Fort Ancient, has been preserved as a state memorial and is a very good example of the Hopewell culture.

There was a later group of mound builders after the Hopewells, but they did not have nearly as much ability as the Hopewells, although we have no way of knowing why. By the time the Europeans first came to Ohio, all these early peoples had vanished as mysteriously as they had come. No one knows the reason.

At about the time the Europeans first knew there was an Ohio region, Indians called the Eries were living in the northern part of the area. The Eries were driven out of Ohio by the fierce Iroquois Indians, but they gave their name to Lake Erie and to the city of Erie, not far from Ohio in Pennsylvania.

Many people have the mistaken idea that the early American countryside was swarming with Indians. The truth is, there were never really very many Indians in Ohio. In all of the area of present-day Ohio, it is likely there were no more than 15,000 Indians. Most of these did not have very permanent locations for their homes.

When this is compared with the more than ten million people who live in Ohio now, it is clear that the Indians were not in very secure possession of the land nor were they making very good use of it.

In all this great Ohio country the Indians were scarcely more than ghosts among the trees. Later Europeans found four principal groups, Wyandot (or Huron), Delaware, Miami, and Shawnee.

CLAIMS AND STRUGGLES FOR A NEW LAND

Europeans may have seen the upper Ohio River and set foot in Ohio before the French explorer La Salle, but there is no record. La Salle is usually considered to be the first European ever in Ohio.

La Salle was sent by the French governor at Quebec on his famous exploration through Ohio in 1669-70. The explorations of La Salle gave the French their claim to the whole Ohio country.

Of course, the English disputed the French claim to the land and set out to see what they could do to get it for themselves.

They sent three men, Conrad Weiser, George Croghan, and Andrew Montour, into Ohio to win the friendship of the Indians. Croghan later became known as the "King of the Traders," and the

Algonquian Village about 1500 A.D.
© 1964, Michigan Bell Telephone Company

many gifts the English gave the Indians helped to win them to the English side.

Meanwhile the French were not idle. They sent their expert, Celeron de Bienville, down the Ohio River with 250 men. It must have been a strange sight. Celeron carried with him a supply of lead plates on which the French claim to the land had been stamped. These lead plates he buried with great ceremony at six places along the Ohio River, hoping that these permanent metal tablets would establish the French rights to the area for all time.

The historian Harlan Hatcher calls Celeron's trip the "most diverting episode in the bloody realism of all our early Ohio history."

Some of these priceless metal plates have been rediscovered in modern times. One of the plates was actually found by Ohio boys swimming in the river near Marietta. Before anyone knew how valuable it was, a part of the plate had been melted to make bullets, but a small piece of it was saved, and can now be seen in a museum in Massachusetts.

The British paid no attention to Celeron's claims and offered 200,000 acres (80,940 hectares) of land in Ohio to the Ohio Company of Virginia if they could settle 100 families in Ohio within seven years.

To explore their land, the Ohio Company sent out an unusual explorer, Christopher Gist of New England. He was to find out the strength and population of the Indians and persuade them to attend a conference to sign a treaty for their Ohio lands.

Gist also was asked to keep a detailed journal of what he found, including the rivers and the best means of navigating them, discover the best passages through the Allegheny Mountains, find the best lands for settlement, and survey and mark their boundaries.

After Gist left New England, on October 31, 1750, and had trav-

Traders and Indians at Camp, *painted by Alfred Jacob Miller.* © *1966, Michigan Bell Telephone Company*

eled a day, the story is told that his dog joined him. The dog had been following a long way behind his master until he thought it would be too late for his master to send him back.

So Gist and his dog pushed on across the Ohio River and over the snow-covered countryside to reach a Wyandot Indian village near the present-day town of Coshocton, on the Muskingum River.

When they reached the Wyandot village, Gist found the Indian's friend, the great trader George Croghan, had established a crude trading post there. Gist stopped in his journey to spend Christmas there and to persuade the Indians to forget the French and become friends with the English.

Christopher Gist kept a careful record of his experiences. He reports that by Christmas morning so much snow had fallen that the Wyandot village was completely snowbound. Croghan's cabin was crowded with traders and Indians, and Gist was reading his Bible. Suddenly he began to read the Christmas story aloud. Everyone was silent. The Indians seemed impressed, and asked their interpreter to repeat the story to them.

Gist felt that the effect was almost like a miracle. Until this time the Indians had been suspicious and unfriendly. Now they even asked him to stay with them and teach them Christianity.

When Gist went on to other Indians, the Wyandots agreed to trade only with the English and gave him a message for the neighboring Indians.

Gist visited the Shawnees and the Miamis, also with great success. On February 25, 1751, the chief of the Miamis said to Christopher Gist, "Brother, we have heard what you have said to us. . . . You may depend upon sincere and true friendship towards you as long as we have strength."

Christopher Gist returned to New England in May. He (and his dog) had recorded and surveyed much of the land north and west of the Ohio River in a journey of 1,200 miles (1,931 kilometers). His description of the country is one of the most interesting we have:

"The Ohio Country is fine, rich, level land, well-timbered with large walnut, ash, sugar trees, cherry trees, etc. It is well watered with a great number of little streams or rivulets, and full of beautiful

19

natural meadows, covered with wild rye, blue grass and clover, and abounds with turkeys, deer, elk and most sorts of game, particularly buffaloes, 30 or 40 of which are frequently seen feeding in one meadow. In short, it wants nothing but cultivation to make it a most delightful country."

WARS AND REBELLIONS

The contest between the British and French grew more bitter until finally it became what is known as the French and Indian War, with the French and the Indians who were friendly to them on one side and the English with their Indian friends on the other.

Of particular interest is the fact that George Washington was sent by the British to defend the Ohio country. He started to build a fort, called Fort Necessity, since it would be necessary to have it finished before the French attacked. However, the French attack came before the roof of Fort Necessity had been finished, and George Washington was forced to give up. This was the only time in the life of this great patriot that he ever surrendered.

To punish the Miami Indians for their friendship with the English, the French destroyed the main Miami village, called Pickawillany.

In spite of their early successes, the French finally lost the war, and the Ohio country came under English control for a short while.

Generally the English attempted to do what was right for the Indians. They established Ohio as an Indian preserve and would not permit any permanent European settlements in it.

In spite of this, many settlers and traders disregarded the Indians' rights by going into the Ohio country against the law.

The Indians were so troubled by this that finally they went on the warpath under the leadership of their great Chief Pontiac. Most of the European settlements and forts in the Ohio country were destroyed. Hundreds of settlers and soldiers were massacred. Many European prisoners were taken.

To keep the Indians in line, Colonel Henry Bouquet gathered an army of 1,500 men. He sent word that all attacks must stop and all

Fort Necessity was reconstructed in 1954.

prisoners be returned. When the Indians saw how large Colonel Bouquet's army was and how well he was training them for Indian warfare, they agreed to accept his conditions.

In 1764 the Indians met Colonel Bouquet near the town of Coshocton to make peace and return their prisoners. A large number of captives of the Indians were returned to their families and friends. The joy of the prisoners at being set free and seeing their families made a wonderfully touching scene, but some of the smallest children had forgotten their families and wanted to stay with the Indians.

This peace was as poorly kept on both sides as the others had been. Finally it was necessary for the governor of Virginia, Lord Dunmore, to lead an army of 2,500 men into Ohio to put down the

Indians once again. This is known as Lord Dunmore's War. When the Indians under Chief Cornstalk were beaten, they gathered to sign a new treaty in 1774.

Near the town of Circleville in Ohio, an enormous elm was preserved as a memorial to one of the Indian chiefs who met to sign this treaty. This was Chief Logan, and the tree has gone down in history as "Logan's Elm." Chief Logan is supposed to have made a famous speech under this elm in which he told of his reasons for going to war with the Europeans.

"I appeal to any white man to say if ever he entered Logan's cabin hungry and I gave him not meat; if ever he came cold or naked and I gave him not clothing.

"During the course of the last long and bloody war, Logan remained in his tent, an advocate for peace. Nay, such was my love for the whites, that those of my own country pointed at me as they passed by and said, 'Logan is the friend of the white man.' I had even thought to live with you, but for the injuries of one man, Colonel Cresap, last spring, in cold blood, and unprovoked, cut off all the relatives of Logan; not sparing even my women and children.

"There runs not a drop of my blood in the veins of any human creature. This called on me for revenge. I have sought it. I have killed many. I have fully glutted my vengeance. For my country, I rejoice at the beams of peace.

"Yet, do not harbor the thought that mine is the joy of fear. Logan never felt fear. He will not turn on his heel to save his life. Who is there to mourn for Logan? Not one."

Logan's oratory was quoted by Thomas Jefferson in his *Notes on the State of Virginia,* and later was quoted in many American and European newspapers.

But peace was still far away. Shortly after Lord Dunmore's War, another and bigger war came to the country. America had declared itself to be independent of England, and the Revolutionary War was being fought.

No important battles of the Revolution were fought in Ohio. Washington had sent men to build Fort Laurens in 1778, near the site of present-day Bolivar, in order to defend the Ohio country from

22

Modern Ohio riflemen recreate the 9th Virginia Regiment for the 1976 Bicentennial.

the British at Detroit. This was the farthest west military post established by George Washington's army.

Much farther west, however, in Illinois and Indiana, the famous American, George Rogers Clark, was fighting the British and Indians, and when he captured Vincennes in Indiana, he made it possible for the Americans to hold the whole Northwest Territory, including Ohio.

In Ohio, most of the war was carried on by the Indians. The British Governor Hamilton paid rewards to the Indians for the scalps of Americans they could bring in during the war. Soon it became difficult to tell who was friend and who was foe.

This situation led to one of the saddest pages in Ohio's history. A group of church people, Moravian missionaries, had started a settlement which they named Schoenbrunn. There they settled a group of Indian families who had been converted to Christianity. These peaceful people refused to take any part in the war.

Angered by this, a group of frontiersmen surprised and captured the colony at near-by Gnadenhutten. After a mock trial, the men, women, and children of the Schoenbrunn colony were murdered. Only two escaped. Ninety-four people died in this senseless massacre.

23

Today Schoenbrunn has been recreated.

When the Indians of Ohio heard of the treatment of the Indians at Schoenbrunn they went on the warpath. General Washington was forced to send his friend Colonel William Crawford to Ohio to try and stop the Indian uprising. Colonel Crawford was captured by the Indians and burned at the stake for revenge.

Finally, of course, the Revolutionary War did come to an end, and the British gave up Ohio and the territory north and west of the Ohio River to the new American country.

AMERICA'S "COLONIES" IN THE NORTHWEST

Ohio and all of the rest of the territory, known as the Northwest, had now become "colonies" of the original thirteen states. The thirteen states were determined that their new colonies would be governed fairly and that they would have a chance to become equal with all the older states as soon as they were ready.

To do this they set up the rules for governing the Northwest Territory in the Northwest Ordinance of 1787. The Ordinance was one of the most skillful and practical sets of laws ever made for governing a new region. It has been called the "Magna Charta of the Northwest."

The Ordinance opened portions of the Northwest Territory, including parts of Ohio, to settlement. Some sections of Ohio were still reserved for the Indians.

Virginia and Connecticut both had long claimed that large parts of Ohio belonged to them and should be governed as actual parts of their states. Other states which had no claims on western lands would not agree to this. Finally Connecticut and Virginia agreed that they would not try to govern their territory in Ohio if they could keep title to a part of the land.

This was agreed, and Connecticut reserved 3,250,000 acres (1,315,230 hectares) in northeastern Ohio, including the site of present-day Cleveland. Connecticut gave tracts of these lands to her citizens who had war damage claims from the Revolutionary War. Many of these people later made their way to their lands in Ohio, so many, in fact, that parts of the region have been called a "second New England." This land was given the name Western Reserve, and the term is still used in many ways in many parts of the region that was the Western Reserve.

Virginia kept title to 4,500,000 acres (1,821,087 hectares) of land in the region between the Scioto and Little Miami rivers and called the area the Virginia Military Survey. This land was given by Virginia to her Revolutionary War veterans as compensation for their services. General George Washington himself received 70,000 acres (28,329 hectares) of this land for his wartime services.

GETTING SETTLED

Another very large tract of Ohio land had been bought by a new Ohio company—The Ohio Company of Associates. This company had been formed in New England in 1787. Their new lands covered

1,500,000 acres (607,029 hectares) and stretched along the Muskingum River from its mouth.

By 1788 the Ohio Company was ready to send a group of 47 people to their new lands in Ohio. They traveled by wagon from their New England homes until they reached the Ohio River, where they built two flatboats, and became the first permanent settlers to float down the Ohio River toward their new homes—as so many thousands would do after them.

Their biggest boat weighed 50 tons (45 metric tons), and as someone has said it "looked like a barn on a raft." When this boat pushed into the shore of the Muskingum River, the settlers were reminded of their Pilgrim forefathers, and their flatboat has been called the "American Mayflower."

A modern version of a keel boat.

Marietta was the name they gave to the new town they built at the spot where the Muskingum and Ohio rivers meet, and it was the first permanent settlement in Ohio. They named the town in honor of Queen Marie Antoinette of France as recognition for the help France had given the colonies during the Revolutionary War.

This group at Marietta was no ordinary group of settlers. They had been carefully chosen and were under the leadership of two outstanding men—the Reverend Manasseh Cutler and General Rufus Putnam.

As George Washington said, "No colony in America was settled under circumstances more favorable. There never were people better able to promote the welfare of the community."

They planned well, had ample money, built an adequate fort for protection against the Indians and before very long had fine homes and thriving activities.

In the same year that Marietta was founded, another small group of settlers also traveled down the Ohio River. They floated on much farther to reach the land which their leader, Benjamin Stites, had explored some time before. They stopped near the mouth of the Miami River, and a little settlement began to grow around Fort Washington there. They called the town Losantiville. Later, when the new governor of the Northwest Territory, General Arthur St. Clair, moved his capital there, he changed the name of Losantiville to Cincinnati.

Soon an amazing throng of people was swarming into the Ohio region. In the year of 1788-89 alone, 10,000 people came to Ohio to settle.

Most of them came floating down the Ohio River on flatboats. This seems like an easy way to travel, and it might have been except for the great danger to travelers on the broad river. Indians lurked almost constantly on the banks, ready to attack the settlers whenever they had a good opportunity. Pirates were as bad or worse. They would lure the settlers to the banks, board the boats, and massacre everyone on board for their property. No one knows how many hundreds or thousands died when their boats were attacked as they were trying to reach their new homes.

Those who did get to the new land found frontier life hard, but they managed to make things somewhat easier for themselves at times by doing some of their work together and helping one another at the more difficult jobs. They cleverly turned some of the work into social gatherings when they met for house raisings, husking bees, barn raisings, house warmings, and apple-butter bees.

These new neighbors, coming in greater and greater numbers, alarmed the Indians. After a new Indian uprising, General Harmer and his army were defeated by Chief Little Turtle in 1790.

In 1791 Governor St. Clair, who was also an army general, set out to protect his territory. He fell into an ambush set by Little Turtle, and 900 of the American soldiers were killed. Governor St. Clair escaped, carrying away eight bullet holes in his clothing. This was one of the worst defeats ever suffered by an American army. Ohio was no longer safe for settlement; the Indians had gained almost complete control.

Alarmed by this situation, President Washington chose the one man he thought could save the Ohio country. He sent General Anthony Wayne to Cincinnati. In the Revolutionary War, General Wayne had been given the nickname of "Mad" Anthony Wayne because people said he took "mad" risks.

In Ohio, however, General Wayne was more careful than "mad." He knew that the training of his men might mean the difference between success or failure. Before fighting Indians it was necessary for the soldiers to learn the strange ways of Indian fighting and how to get along in wilderness country.

The general spent almost a year drilling his troops and giving them the fine points of Indian fighting.

Choosing the very spot where Governor St. Clair had been defeated a while before, General Wayne built a fort which he called Fort Recovery, because he hoped it would assure the recovery of the government's power. He also built Fort Defiance, defying the "English, the Indians and all the devils in hell to take it."

The Indians, encouraged by their British friends, attacked Fort Recovery, using the same methods that defeated Governor St. Clair, but this time they were defeated.

Above: Pioneer conditions live again in modern restorations.
Below: The art of weaving is preserved at restored Schoenbrunn.

Finally the American army and the Indians met in a woodland where a great many trees had been blown down in a storm. A fierce battle took place among these fallen trees and has been given the name the Battle of Fallen Timbers.

Daring General "Mad" Anthony Wayne won a great victory over an army that was probably the largest Indian army ever gathered against the Americans.

Now General Wayne could compel the Indians to assemble to sign

Treaty of Green Ville *by Howard Chandler Christy.*

a peace treaty. A thousand Indians came to Green Ville (now called Greenville) for a conference lasting for two months. Out of this meeting grew the Treaty of Green Ville in 1795. The Indians gave up three-fourths of their Ohio lands, and there never again was an Indian uprising in the state, although the Indians played a considerable part in the War of 1812.

Ohio was now really in a position to grow. In 1800 Congress set Ohio apart as a separate territory, although the name given to it was still that of "Northwest Territory."

By 1803 it was clear that Ohio qualified to become a state. The population was rapidly approaching 70,000.

This growth must be considered to be one of the amazing facts of American history. In 1787 not a single permanent settlement existed in the whole of Ohio. Just 15 years later, almost 70,000 people made their homes there, and Congress was ready for a bill to declare Ohio a state.

Ohio entered the Union as the 17th state in 1803, the first state created west of the Alleghenies.

*Aaron Burr, painted by
James Van Dyke.*

*General "Mad" Anthony
Wayne, attributed to
John Sharples.*

Yesterday and Today

A STATE GOES THROUGH ITS TEENS

Dr. Edward Tiffin was the first governor of Ohio, with his capital at Chillicothe, where it remained until 1808. The square stone capitol built at Chillicothe was the first permanent public building in Ohio.

About this time the people of Cincinnati marveled at a strange sight they saw on the Ohio River, a new kind of boat almost completely surrounded by a cloud of wood smoke. The first steamboat, *New Orleans,* had come to Cincinnati in 1811, and the young town would never be the same again. With its paddles churning the water on either side, the *New Orleans* could bring to Cincinnati the trade of all the rivers from as far away as the city which also had the name New Orleans, in distant Louisiana.

It was not long after the coming of the first steamboat until Cincinnati began to grow into her new title, which she kept for so long— "Queen City of the West."

This period saw also the beginning of the great "National Road." Starting in Cumberland, Maryland, the road ran for its longest part through Ohio, connecting Cambridge, Zanesville, Columbus, and Springfield. This road was completed in 1840 and is now marked U.S. Highway 40. Those who travel the road today will be interested to see some of the original highway markers of the old road, which still remain in various locations.

In this early period of statehood, Ohio played a key part in one of the strangest stories of United States history. Aaron Burr had been a leading figure in America, a vice-president of the United States, and missed being president by only one vote.

Burr lost his great public following as the result of his fatal duel with Alexander Hamilton. However, Burr never gave up hope of becoming a powerful figure once again. He continued to plan for his return to public life in one way or another. Some people felt that his plans were nothing more than plots against the U.S. government.

This was the man who in 1805 first visited Blennerhasset Island in the Ohio River near Marietta. He found the island an amazing place, the home of wealthy Harman Blennerhasset. The Blennerhassets lived in the beautiful home they had built on this 175-acre (71-hectare) island, and the whole island had been amazingly developed.

Burr did not stay long on his first visit to Blennerhasset, but the place had made a strong impression on him. He returned later with his beautiful and famous daughter, Theodosia, for a longer stay. He had bought a very large tract of land in the new Louisiana territory; so he said he would build a fleet of boats to take goods and settlers to his new land. Burr ordered the building of 15 large boats on the Muskingum River above Marietta.

To the federal government, Burr appeared to be building a naval fleet to set himself up as a ruler in some of the U.S. territories.

At the urging of President Jefferson, the Ohio legislature passed a law for the "immediate arrest of anyone fitting out a vessel or marching armed persons through Ohio with an intention hostile to the peace and welfare of the U.S."

Burr and his friend Blennerhasset were arrested and tried, but the government had no proof that they were traitors, and they were freed. To this day no one is sure what Aaron Burr's real intentions were when he made his plans at Blennerhasset Island and built his boats in Ohio.

ANOTHER ROUND WITH ENGLAND

Relations of the young American country with Great Britain had grown steadily worse over a period of years until in 1812 another war broke out. Ohio was to have a key part in this War of 1812, and a future Ohio resident would make such a great reputation that he would become the first president of the United States from Ohio.

This man was William Henry Harrison. Early in the war he had been assigned to capture Detroit from the English. Starting out from Cincinnati, Harrison marched toward Detroit. By this time Ohio was not all the wilderness it had been at the time Harrison learned how to fight the Indians under General "Mad" Anthony Wayne.

34

When the War of 1812 began, the population of Ohio had reached the unbelievable figure of 240,000, almost four times as many people as there had been only nine years before when Ohio became a state.

For the defense of Ohio, Harrison built Fort Meigs, named for the wartime governor of Ohio whose unusual name was Return Jonathan Meigs. Fort Meigs was a great success. Twice the British and their Indian allies besieged Fort Meigs, but they could never take it. The fort was so strong it was given the nickname "Gibralter of the North."

One of the Indians who fought with the British at Fort Meigs was the fierce and famous Chief Tecumseh, who had been given the rank of major in the British army. Tecumseh is usually considered to be one of the really great Indian chieftains. At a battle on the Raisin River, which the Americans lost, the British General Proctor was permitting the Americans to be massacred when Tecumseh stopped the killing, shouting, "For shame! Desist; it is a disgrace to kill a defenseless prisoner."

Not all of the Indians were unfriendly to Americans. In order to be certain of where the Indians stood, General Harrison called a great council of the friendly Indians in 1813. These Indians, led by Tarhe the Crane, Chief of the Wyandots, agreed to stay neutral. This relieved much of the pressure from the American forces.

One of the most stirring battles of the War of 1812 took place at a small, strong place called Fort Stephanson, near Fremont. When the British under General Proctor attacked the fort, commanded by Major George Croghan, there were only 150 Americans to fend off 1,200 of the enemy. Major Croghan managed to hold out against these terrible odds. The British were defeated, and General Proctor left the fight.

Major Croghan had only one cannon, which he gave the friendly nickname of "Old Betsy." Today at the foot of Fort Stephanson monument in Fremont, visitors will still find Old Betsy ready to defend her Ohio countryside.

Only one major sea battle took place on the Great Lakes. The British controlled the Lakes with a fleet of six strong warships. Captain

Oliver Hazard Perry had a plan to capture the waters of the Great Lakes from the British. When he received permission to try his plan, he brought 50 ship carpenters and a master shipbuilder to Erie, Pennsylvania, in March of 1813. Only four months later his men had completed nine fully stocked and armed warships.

Off the Ohio shore at Put-in-Bay in September of 1813, the British fleet and the new American fleet met in battle. In the fierce fighting of the Battle of Put-in-Bay, Perry's flagship was put out of service. The dauntless captain merely wrapped his ship's flag around him, rowed to another ship and continued the battle.

When the British surrendered, Perry made one of the most famous of all war-time statements, his well-remembered announcement, "We have met the enemy, and they are ours!"

Battle of Lake Erie *by William Powell.*

*Perry's Victory and International Peace Memorial stands
at Put-in-Bay on South Bass Island in Lake Erie.*

The Battle of Put-in-Bay proved to be the last battle of the War of 1812 in Ohio. General William Henry Harrison, who had helped Perry plan the naval victory, went on with his forces into Canada and defeated the British at the Battle of the Thames River, where Chief Tecumseh was killed.

GROWING LIKE A MUSHROOM

Now Ohio was no longer a cluster of small communities huddled near forts along the river banks. All parts of the state were rapidly growing and developing. The state needed a centrally located capital. With this in mind, the capital of Ohio was moved to Columbus in 1816, where it has been ever since.

When the first steamboat, with the picturesque name of *Walk-in-the-Water,* began to operate on Lake Erie in 1818, the harbors of the north were able to take another large step toward becoming great ports of trade.

Another interesting event was the founding of the community of Zoar on the Tuscarawas River in Tuscarawas County. This community was set up in 1817 by a German group who had left their home country because of persecution for their religious faith.

When they reached their 5,500 acres (2,226 hectares) of mortgaged land in Ohio, they realized that they could not pay their debts within the required 15 years without working together. So they pooled all their property and wealth and formed a new organization that they called the Society of Separatists of Zoar, directed by an elected board of trustees. Men and women had equal rights, and all were required to work for the common good at whatever job they were assigned. Soon they had fine homes, beautiful gardens, orchestras, bands and choirs, and found life enjoyable. By 1853 their assets were valued at more than $1,000,000.

The community garden of Zoar was one of the show places of the state. It has been restored and can still be seen today.

Later Zoarites became discontented, and the society was finally dissolved in 1898.

38

Old Zoar comes to life once again.

Another prominent religious group made their homes in Ohio. Their stay was shorter than that of the Zoarites, but their influence can still be felt. In 1831 Joseph Smith, the leader of the Church of Jesus Christ of Latter Day Saints, came with his family to live in Kirtland. These Mormons, as they were called, grew rapidly in number. Some estimates show that there were as many as 20,000 Mormons in Ohio. They were often misunderstood and their religious beliefs made many people dislike them, so in 1838 the leaders moved to Missouri with most of their followers.

In 1835 Ohio experienced its "Border War." The boundary between Ohio and Michigan had never been fixed exactly. Both states claimed the border territory between them. Just when it looked as though the two states might actually go to war to settle their claims, President Andrew Jackson sent a representative to persuade both governors to settle the dispute peacefully.

Fortunately, they did just that. Because Ohio was given the disputed territory, Michigan received the whole "Upper Peninsula" to make up for it.

When William Henry Harrison, Ohio hero of the War of 1812, became a candidate for president of the United States in 1840, his friends in Ohio made every effort to help him win. One of his opponents said that Harrison would be much better sitting in front of his log cabin than he would be in the White House.

This brought about the "Log Cabin" campaign. Harrison supporters had log cabins made out of Ohio buckeye wood. They mounted the cabins on wagons and toured every part of the state with parades and rallies for the "Log Cabin Candidate." The buckeye wood cabins made such an impression and Harrison's supporters passed out so many canes made of buckeye wood that people from Ohio came to be called "Buckeyes." Ever since that time Ohio has been called the Buckeye State, and the buckeye is the official state tree. The buckeye is a kind of horse chestnut. Its nut has a white spot that the Indians thought looked like the eye of a buck, so they called it buck-eye.

General Harrison was successful in his campaign, and Ohio had a favorite son in the White House. Regrettably, President Harrison died of pneumonia in 1841, little more than a month after taking office.

One of the most important events of peaceful days in Ohio was the coming of the railroad in 1848. That first railroad operated between Dayton and Sandusky.

The rise of the railroads marked the end of the great influence of canals in Ohio. The Ohio and Erie Canal, between Cleveland and

Today's visitors can still recapture the flavor of the historic canal days by riding on the canal boat William Henry Harrison *at the Piqua historical area.*

Portsmouth, had been completed in 1832. In 1843 the Miami and Erie Canal opened. Canals were busy trade routes in Ohio, but only for about 25 years.

ABOLITIONISTS AND COPPERHEADS

Whether men should be slaves or free was the question that rapidly began to divide Americans in the years before 1860. Many Ohio people, mostly in southern Ohio, felt that slavery was right. They were called Copperheads. More Ohioans thought that slavery was wrong; the ones who felt most strongly about this were labeled Abolitionists.

Many prominent Abolitionists lived in Ohio. John Brown, who was later hanged for attacking an arsenal of the federal government, made a fortune as a wool merchant in Cincinnati. He was one of the country's greatest experts on wool when he left Ohio for New England, where he hoped to corner the wool market and become even more rich and powerful. His failure to do this and the loss of his fortune were probably strong reasons for his later bitterness and possibly helped to bring on his wild actions against slavery.

John Rankin was another of Ohio's strongest Abolitionists. His home on the banks of the Ohio River near Cincinnati was one of the important stations on the "Underground Railroad." This was the name given to the route used by slaves who escaped from their masters and fled into Canada. Many people risked large fines and prison sentences to help the blacks escape.

As many as 12 escaping slaves are said to have been sheltered at one time in John Rankin's small house. He is supposed to have watched a slave girl named Eliza escape across the ice of the Ohio River, carrying her baby in her arms. After reaching the Ohio side, they are reported to have been sheltered in the Rankin house.

A prominent woman living in Cincinnati, Harriet Beecher Stowe, had visited at John Rankin's home and had heard his accounts of helping the slaves on the Underground Railroad and of Eliza crossing the ice.

On to Liberty, *a painting by Theodor Kaufmann*
dramatizes the tensions of escape for the slaves.

Mrs. Stowe was no longer living in Ohio when she wrote her famous book about Eliza and her escape, but most of the information about slavery in *Uncle Tom's Cabin* was gained while Harriet Beecher Stowe lived in Cincinnati, where slavery and the escape of slaves were constant topics. This book is said to have done more to bring on the crisis about slavery than any other one thing.

BROTHER AGAINST BROTHER

That crisis soon came, and the young American nation was divided by Civil War, with even families divided, brother fighting against brother.

Ohio troops took part in the first land battle of the Civil War at Philippi in present-day West Virginia.

Then in August, 1862, it appeared that Ohio, itself, would be invaded. Southern troops were threatening Cincinnati. Governor David Tod called on all Ohio civilian men who were able to respond. He placed General Lew Wallace in command of the defense of Cincinnati. General Wallace, then only 25 years old, later was known throughout the world for his famous novel *Ben Hur.* This book had one of the greatest successes of any novel and also was made into several important motion pictures.

There was an amazing response to Governor Tod's request for fighters. Office workers, mechanics, farmers, businessmen—all answered the call, a total of 15,766. They came so quickly and in such casual clothes that people said they looked like "Squirrel Hunters."

The enemy never came within sight of the trenches the Squirrel Hunters had hastily dug to defend Cincinnati. In September, Governor Tod was able to write to the Secretary of War, Stanton:

"The minute-men or Squirrel Hunters responded gloriously to the call for the defense of Cincinnati. Thousands reached the city, and thousands more were en route for it. The enemy having retreated, all have been ordered back. This uprising of the people is the cause of the retreat. You should acknowledge publicly this gallant conduct. Please order Quartermaster Burr to pay all transportation bills, upon my approval."

The Ohio General Assembly later adopted this resolution: "Resolved . . . that the Governor is hereby authorized and directed to appropriate out of his contingent fund, a sufficient sum to pay for the printing and lithographing discharges to the patriotic men of the State, who responded to the call of the Governor and went to the southern border to repel the invader, and who will be known in history as the Squirrel Hunters."

Although Cincinnati was never invaded, other parts of Ohio were not to escape so easily. The first invasion of Ohio took place in 1862 when Confederate General Albert Jenkins swept into the state with a small group of men. He did little damage and the raid had no lasting effect.

The raid of John Hunt Morgan across a wide sweep of Ohio in

1863 was a different matter. There were at least forty-nine Ohio towns that suffered from Morgan's attacks, which have been called the "most spectacular raids of the Civil War." Finally, Morgan and his men were captured at Salineville. But Morgan himself escaped to carry on his efforts for the Confederacy. Morgan's raids in Ohio were the northernmost fighting of the Civil War.

Another raid of a different kind was interesting to Ohio because Ohioans formed most of the force. This was Andrews' Raid.

General Ormsby M. Mitchel directed the raid from Cincinnati. He had selected James J. Andrews to lead a group deep into the South to destroy as many railroads and railroad bridges as possible. The raiders filtered into the South in civilian clothes, but before they accomplished much most of them had been captured, some were imprisoned or executed as spies, while a few escaped to return to Ohio. They had managed to steal a locomotive and raced it up the tracks, pursued by Confederates in another locomotive. Of course, this is the reason Andrews' Raid has gone down in history as the "Great Locomotive Chase."

Andrews was hanged at Atlanta, but while his mission was a failure, six of his men, all Ohioans, were the first men to receive the Congressional Medal of Honor, which had just been established. In all, 144 Ohioans received the Congressional Medal of Honor for heroic service during the Civil War.

One of the strangest happenings of the Civil War in Ohio was what has been called the Lake Erie Conspiracy. This became one of the sensations of the war in late 1864. A group of Confederate leaders under Captain Charles Cole planned to capture the only warship on the Great Lakes, the U.S.S. *Michigan,* stationed in the Bay of Sandusky. They hoped to use the ship to free nearby Southern prisoners and set up a Confederate stronghold at Sandusky.

This plot might have succeeded if Cole had not been betrayed by one of the Confederate prisoners. Cole was tried but he never was sent to the firing squad. He received a presidential pardon and afterward went to Texas to be a rancher.

At last, of course, the war ended. Ohio had sent 345,000 men to the Union army. Now those who were alive were coming home.

William Tecumseh Sherman was one of the most colorful generals of the Civil War. A Lancaster native, he graduated from West Point. His fame after the war was such that he might have become President, but he refused even to be considered for the post. Left: Artist Andrew B. Carlin produced this naive painting showing Sherman's famous march to the sea.

President Abraham Lincoln was going home, too. The wartime president had been murdered, and his funeral train moved somberly across Ohio toward his old home in Springfield, Illinois, while all Ohio mourned. Saddened crowds lined the railroad tracks all the way.

BASEBALLS AND ATOMS

After the war, many people sought recreation, and baseball came into prominence. Ohio can claim to be the home of the first professional baseball team, the Cincinnati Red Stockings, founded in 1866. The team had the unusual distinction of winning every game in its first season.

Second Great Match for the Championship *by John L. Magee.*

Cincinnati in the 1870s by Warren and Wellstood.

Ohio has had some most-distinguished baseball men. Cy Young won more games than any other pitcher in history, 511. Bill Wambsganss of the Cleveland Indians made an unassisted triple play. Johnny Vander Meer of the Cincinnati Reds is the only pitcher ever to have pitched two no-hit games in succession.

The city of Cincinnati itself holds a record in another field. Cincinnati needed a railroad into the South. Much of their former trade was going in other directions. So the city undertook to do what no city had ever tried before—to build and operate a whole railroad. In 1880 Cincinnati finished the Southern Railroad.

Just one hundred years after its founding, the city of Cincinnati celebrated with a Centennial exposition in 1888. The Machinery Hall at this exposition was three blocks long. It had been built over a canal, and gondolas were imported from Italy to glide the length of the building on the canal.

During this period the whole state was gaining a reputation for invention, manufacturing, and industry. John D. Rockefeller had formed the Standard Oil Company at Cleveland in 1870. The cash register had been invented in Dayton by James Ritty in 1879, and the National Cash Register Company was formed there.

L.E. Custer invented the electric runabout at Dayton in 1899. The Wright brothers carried out most of their experiments near Dayton, although their first flight was at Kitty Hawk, NC. In 1901 the

Wrights built the first wind tunnel for aeronautical testing, at Dayton. Charles Kettering invented the automatic self-starter at Dayton in 1909.

One of the worst floods in Ohio history swept down the Ohio Valley in 1913. Five hundred people died and property damage amounted to 300 million dollars. This flood brought about one of the finest conservation efforts ever undertaken by a state. The Ohio state legislature passed the Conservancy Act in 1914. This called for the building of a series of flood control dams on the various rivers of the Ohio watershed. Flood control experts from all over the world have studied the results of this early successful effort to keep the rivers within their banks and to keep rich soil from running off the land.

World War I was fought far from Ohio, but 200,000 men went into service from Ohio and many never returned. James M. Cox was Ohio's wartime governor, and Newton D. Baker of Cleveland served as Secretary of War in President Wilson's cabinet.

After the war two disasters hit Ohio. One of these was man-made, the great depression beginning in 1929. The other was the great flood of 1937, which has been called the worst flood in the history of the Ohio River. In many cities the crest of the Ohio's flood was the highest ever recorded.

World War II called for the services of more Ohio men and women than any other war in its history. Eight hundred and forty thousand Ohioans were in uniform, and Ohio played its part in later wars as well.

Important modern developments in Ohio have included the establishment in 1952 of the Portsmouth Area Project to produce uranium 235 for atomic work, the opening of the Ohio Turnpike in 1955 and the opening of the first titanium roll and forge plant in the country at Toronto in 1956.

When the St. Lawrence Seaway was finally opened in 1959, ocean boats of large size could come up the seaway into the Great Lakes. This meant that at last Ohio's great ports had become "seaports."

In 1969 Ohio's astronaut, Neil Armstrong, became one of the most noted explorers in history, first man to step on the moon.

48

The port of Toledo

During the decade of the 1970s, a state income tax was established in 1971. In politics, another famous astronaut, John Glenn, won an Ohio seat in the United States Senate in 1974, while in 1977 Howard Metzenbaum assumed the Senate seat held by Robert Taft, Jr., of the famous Taft family.

Natural Treasures

TREASURES FROM THE EARTH

Ohio is not a large state; 35 of the 50 states are larger than Ohio, but in the relatively small area of Ohio there is a great assembly of the treasures that are necessary to life in modern times.

The soil itself is one of Ohio's greatest treasures. Much of the land was covered with a variety of rich soils brought by the glaciers and left by them as a gift to the state.

Beneath the soil, the greatest treasure is the supply of coal. About 21 billion tons (19 billion metric tons) of coal are still in deposits in Ohio.

This is the base on which much of the wealth and industry of the state has been built. Millions of tons of coal come from the Ohio strip mines each year. In southeastern and eastern Ohio visitors find much to interest them in the strip mining operations, where giant shovels may gulp up almost 100 tons (91 metric tons) of coal at a single bite.

A pipeline that actually carries coal in powdered form for 108 miles (174 kilometers), from Cadiz to Cleveland, is another of the unique features of the Ohio coal country.

Although oil and natural gas have been taken from the Ohio reserves since before the Civil War, there are still 121 million barrels (16 million metric tons) available in Ohio according to current estimates. Ohio reserves include more than a billion cubic feet (28 million cubic meters) of natural gas, which flows to the consumers through 10,000 miles (16,000 kilometers) of pipeline.

Limestone and sandstone are two of the most important riches of the state. Near Barberton, a limestone mine half a mile deep (.8 kilometer) is said to be the deepest in the world, while the world's largest sandstone quarry has been developed at South Amherst.

Almost innumerable uses of limestone and dolomite are found in

Opposite: Sunset over the harbor of Put-in-Bay.

*Stackers build and then reclaim iron ore and limestone
from piles at the Pittsburgh Conneaut facility.*

construction, agriculture, ceramics, glass making, metallurgy and steel making, and cement. Ohio's much admired capitol building was constructed of gray limestone quarried not far from Columbus, not many miles from its site. The figure is a little difficult to grasp, but Ohio produces a mammoth two-thirds of all the sandstone used for building in the United States.

So much of the world's finest clay is found in Ohio that the state leads all others in producing clay products. Brick making began at the first settlement in Marietta, and some of the original brick buildings there can still be seen. Colorful pottery making got its start in Cincinnati in 1799.

Although Ohio ranks only fifth in salt production, the rock salt beds of northeast Ohio could furnish all the salt needed by the United States for 150,000 years. Salt production is likely the oldest industry in the state, with the Indians evaporating the salt from saline springs before the coming of the Europeans. Today more salt is used in the great chemical industry than is used to flavor foods.

Ohio's importance in quarrying is emphasized by the Mac-o-Cheek Castle in West Liberty.

LIVING TREASURES

When the pioneers came to Ohio they found wonderful forests, mostly of hardwoods, covering almost 95 percent of the state. They considered this wealth a hardship, since most of the trees had to be cut down with great labor to clear the land for farming.

Today only about 14 percent of Ohio is forested. Most of the state's lumber comes from second-growth woodlots, but there are many reforestation projects under way.

Almost no large wild animals roam Ohio today, with the exception of deer. Rabbits, squirrels, red foxes, opossums, woodchucks, and other small mammals are found. One hundred and ninety-four kinds of birds nest in Ohio, and 170 species of fish swim in the waters of the state.

The People Use Their Treasures

PUTTING THE SOIL TO USE

At one time, most of the people of Ohio received their living from farming. Today a constantly decreasing percentage farms.

In past years Ohio led all states in the production of corn. Now corn is still an important crop, but Ohio is presently only on the far eastern edge of the corn belt. Ohio is third in U.S. production of popcorn, and, surprisingly, is fifth in maple syrup. The center of maple syrup production is at Chardon. Oats, soybeans, and winter wheat are other important crops. Most people would be surprised to learn that Ohio ranks 10th in tobacco production, and even produces a substantial quantity of sugar beets. The state is sixth in grape production, which is used by wineries.

Ohio ranks high in one unusual kind of "agriculture." Ohio has the third largest area anywhere of greenhouses for growing vegetables, constantly under glass. Among other crops, this greenhouse area produces nearly half of all the U.S. hothouse tomatoes. The state also is a leader in the growing of flowers under glass, with over 1,000 greenhouses for flowers.

Agriculture is a multi-billion dollar a year industry. Dairy products account for about 20 percent of that income, hogs 17 percent, cattle 15 percent, and poultry 11 percent.

A STATE THAT MAKES THINGS

Only two other states produced more value of manufactured products than Ohio. This record makes the state one of the great manufacturing centers of the world. Possibly no other state has its manufacturing so evenly spread throughout its area or produces a wider variety of products.

Opposite: Fresh sweet corn destined for Toledo and Detroit markets is prepared for shipment in Swanton.

Ohio's young people are encouraged to continue in the important occupation of agriculture.

An Akron man, Benjamin Franklin Goodrich, had a vision of the great future of rubber if somehow it could be made stronger and would hold its shape. Dr. Goodrich was able to persuade 19 Akron men to take a chance with him on his new process, called vulcanization, and invest $1,000 each. They started by making rubber fire hose, wringer rolls, and beverage tubing. From this small beginning, Akron has grown to what is now called the "Rubber Capital of the World."

Cleveland was an early center for great industrial development. When John D. Rockefeller established his enormous Standard Oil Company there, Cleveland became in a sense the oil capital of the country. The companies of Thomas A. Edison and Charles F. Brush, who lighted Public Square in Cleveland with his new carbon arc lamp, were combined to form the giant General Electric Company at Nela Park in East Cleveland.

By 1900 Cleveland had become a major center for auto manufacturing. Six major automobile companies were in production in Cleveland. At one time 80 different automobiles were manufactured there. Although most of the industry later moved to Detroit, Cleveland still is important in the manufacture of auto bodies, accessories and parts, plate glass, and sheet steel.

56

Actually, a Cleveland man, Charles B. Shanks, a writer for the Cleveland newspaper the *Plain Dealer,* is credited with coining the very word "automobile" itself.

Cincinnati should be one of the world's cleanest cities. It is an international center for soap manufacturing. Ivorydale has been a soap leader since it began to sell to the federal government in the Civil War.

Its famous floating soap was discovered by accident. A worker is said to have gone off to his lunch without turning off a mixer. The batch of soap he was working on became filled with bubbles of air, but no one knew this had happened, so they wrapped the soap up and shipped it off to their customers as if there had been no change. Then orders began to stream in from people who wanted more of this wonderful soap because it would float, and it has been selling that way ever since.

Cincinnati is also a center for playing card production and is one of the world's leaders for an extremely important kind of production, the manufacturing of machine tools.

Ohio is one of the leading producers of glass of all kinds, from the Bohemian glass making of the 1800s to the modern production of such products as glass fiber and tumblers. A factory at Bellaire is one of the few producers anywhere of fine colored glass and milk glass.

Working with glass

One of the largest producers of cheese, Ohio has at Van Wert one of the biggest cheese factories anywhere, and Ohio makes all the Leiderkranz brand cheese in the world.

Youngstown was once a vital center of Ohio's steel and aluminum production. The steel industry in Ohio started in 1804 at Heaton's Hopewell furnace, near Poland.

Toledo is the home of the Jeep and Toledo scales. Still another leading product of Ohio is the vacuum cleaner. Herbert W. Hoover started to make vacuum cleaners at Canton when the coming of the automobile cut down orders for saddles at his leather plant. Before long, the vacuum had practically displaced his leather business.

Ohio's important steel mills are located in the Cleveland-Lorain and Youngstown areas.

A STATE THAT DOES THINGS

Another kind of activity not generally associated with Ohio was fishing. The richest freshwater area for commercial fishing to be found anywhere at one time was in the waters of Lake Erie off the Ohio shore. Each year many millions of pounds were caught. Sandusky became one of the leading fishing ports of the world, but the industry has dwindled.

Another port, the Port of Cleveland, handles more iron ore than any other shipping center. In another field of transportation, the Ohio Turnpike has become one of the nation's greatest highways, and Wright-Patterson Field is one of the great flight and aviation centers of the world.

Although its beginning in railroading seems small, Ohio had more miles of railroads during the Civil War than any other state, only a few years after the first railroads came. Ohio still ranks high in railroad mileage and business.

The great communications industry in Ohio got its start with the first newspaper published north of the Ohio River. The *Sentinel of the Northwest Territory* was first published in 1793. Today Ohio publishers rank high among the leaders in producing magazines and books.

The Allegheny steam engine.

Six of Ohio's presidents: top, James A. Garfield and Ulysses S. Grant; center, William G. Harding; and bottom, William H. Harrison, Rutherford B. Hayes, and William McKinley.

Human Treasures

"MOTHER OF PRESIDENTS"

Along with Virginia, Ohio claims first rank in having contributed more presidents of the United States than any other. Eight native-born Virginians and seven native-born Ohioans have become president, and William Henry Harrison is usually considered an Ohioan although he was not born in Ohio.

Five of Ohio's presidents were also generals in the Civil War. Three Ohio men immediately succeeded one another as president— Ulysses S. Grant, Rutherford B. Hayes, and James A. Garfield, the 18th, 19th, and 20th presidents.

Ulysses Simpson Grant was born at Point Pleasant, Ohio. He was not really "U.S." Grant at all. His name was Hiram Ulysses Grant, but Congressman Thomas L. Hamer of Georgetown hurriedly made out the recommendation for Grant's appointment to West Point on the last day of the Congressman's term of office. He put down Ulysses S. Grant, because he thought Grant had been given his mother's family name of Simpson, and so the new name was the one that went down in history.

The small rented cottage where Grant was born is now a state memorial building at Point Pleasant, and attracts visitors from all over the country as a historical shrine. When Grant's father went into his own tannery business he built a larger house, of brick, for his family in the fall of 1823. Ulysses attended the Presbyterian Academy at Ripley, Ohio, before going on to West Point. Ulysses did not live in Ohio after that time.

Born in Delaware, Ohio, in 1822, Rutherford B. Hayes began his career practicing law in Fremont. In the Civil War he rose to the rank of general, and during that war, while he was still in service, he was elected to Congress. He refused to leave the battlefield, but after the war he served his term and was reelected. In 1876 he became the Republican candidate for president. Because the election had been contested, he was not declared the duly elected president until just three days before the inauguration was scheduled, March 5, 1877.

The home of Rutherford B. Hayes.

As president, Hayes concluded the federal government's postwar reconstruction of the South and paved the way for the permanent civil service program. After the presidency, Hayes returned to his beautiful estate near Fremont, Spiegel Grove. This estate was donated to Ohio as a memorial and today it is open to the public.

Every day of his long life Hayes kept a record of his activities. This is one of the great personal records of this country in the nineteenth century and is a prized possession of the Rutherford B. Hayes Library, also a part of the Hayes Memorial. There, too, is found the simple monument marking the tomb of the 19th president and his wife.

James A. Garfield, born in Orange, near Cleveland, first gained national attention as a successful Union general in the Civil War. He served as a Congressman and was elected to the presidency, taking office in 1881. In July of that same year the president was passing through the railroad station in Washington when he was shot by an assassin. He lingered for 10 weeks and died in September, 1881.

A grandson of Ohio's first president, William Henry Harrison, Benjamin Harrison, was born near North Bend, Ohio. He became the 23rd president of the United States. Although he grew up in Ohio and received his education from Miami University at Oxford, Ohio, he went on to Indianapolis to practice law, and actually went to the presidency from Indiana.

William McKinley was born in Niles, Ohio, January 29, 1843. He began his career as a teacher, served with distinction in the Civil War, became an attorney in Canton, Ohio, and became a Congressman. He served in the House of Representatives at Washington for 14 years, then for four years as governor of Ohio. On March 4, 1897, William McKinley became the 25th president of the United States.

When the Spanish American War broke out, McKinley led the country to victory in only five months. It was President McKinley who established American policies toward the new territories which came under American control after the war, avoiding the creation of a United States empire.

The country reelected McKinley to the presidency in 1900. In the fall of 1901 he went to the World's Fair at Buffalo to make a speech.

After the speech the president stood in a reception line. As he

Troop C, Ninth Ohio U.S. Cavalry volunteers, with Captain Taylor leading the charge at San Juan, Puerto Rico, during the Spanish-American War.

offered his hand to a man who was wearing a bandage, the man pulled a gun from the bandage and shot the Chief Executive twice. The president died within a week. The nation has seldom been so shocked. "President McKinley was sincerely loved by many, and admired by the people at large for his integrity and effectiveness in public office and for the faultlessness of his private life."

Only six years after his death a magnificent memorial was dedicated to the memory of President McKinley at Canton, Ohio. The mausoleum is 97 feet (30 meters) high and 75 feet (23 meters) across. A bronze statue of the president shows him as he delivered his last speech at Buffalo. The memorial cost $560,000, which was raised by public subscription.

The seventh president from Ohio, William Howard Taft, was elected in 1908. He was born in Cincinnati, where the Tafts have been a leading family for many years. William Howard Taft has the unique distinction in American history to be the only man who has ever served as president of the United States and also as Chief Justice of the United States—the two highest offices in the land.

Charles Taft, half-brother of William Howard, and Mrs. Taft, donated the beautiful Taft home in Cincinnati and their art collection to the people of Cincinnati, and the home where William Howard Taft was born in 1857 is also preserved as a memorial.

Robert A. Taft, son of the president, was elected to the U.S. Senate in 1939, becoming so prominent in Republican Party affairs that he was often called "Mr. Republican." His early death in 1953 cut short a brilliant career.

The third generation of the Taft family to play a prominent part in national politics is Robert Taft, son of Robert A. Taft, who was elected to Congress in 1962.

The last Ohioan so far to become president of the United States was Warren Gamaliel Harding, born near Blooming Grove, Ohio, in 1865. In private life he was a newspaper man. He served in the Ohio Senate, was lieutenant governor of the state and went to the U.S.

Opposite: Robert Taft in a medallion portrait by Deane Keller.

TAFT

Senate in 1914. In 1920 Warren G. Harding was elected the 29th president. Strangely enough, his Democratic opponent for the presidency, James M. Cox, of Dayton, was also an Ohioan, and also a newspaperman. After a long illness, President Harding died in office at San Francisco in 1923.

It is a sad fact that of the six American presidents who have died in office, three were Ohioans, and two of these were assassinated.

"MOTHER OF INVENTORS"

"Ohio brought the world both light and flight," is a phrase often used to describe the unusual contribution which Ohioans have made to science and invention.

A man who is generally recognized to have been one of the most productive inventors of all time, Thomas Alva Edison, was born in Milan, Ohio, in 1847. Most of his important work was done in laboratories in the East, but Ohio still claims him as a son.

The story of two unknown brothers from Dayton, Ohio, who neglected their bicycle shop to experiment with flying machines, is known to everyone. Wilbur and Orville Wright built the world's first successful powered heavier-than-air flying machine. While their first flight did not take place in Ohio, most of their research and development work, both earlier and later, took place in the Dayton vicinity.

We have already seen how two other inventors helped to make Dayton an unusual center of invention: James Ritty and his cash register and L.E. Custer and his electric runabout. Charles F. Kettering gained his first national reputation with the invention of the automatic self-starter. With a group of associates, Mr. Kettering founded the Dayton Engineering Laboratories Company. This became one of the country's leading research organizations and under Mr. Kettering's direction such improvements as high-octane gasoline were developed. The firm soon became known by its initials, D-E-L-CO, and when it joined the General Motors organization it became the DELCO division.

Above: Thomas A. Edison's portrait by Abraham A. Anderson, showing the inventor with the second model of his phonograph featuring wax cylinder records. Below: The Wright brothers invented the airplane in the back of this bicycle shop, now at Greenfield Village near Detroit.

Another famed Ohio inventor was Charles Martin Hall, who discovered the method of making aluminum with electricity, upon which the modern aluminum industry is based.

"MOTHER OF GENERALS"

In addition to the generals from Ohio who have already been mentioned, the state produced a great number of other wartime leaders. The three Civil War generals usually ranked first, second, and third among the Union generals were from Ohio—Grant, of course, and then Sherman and Sheridan.

William Tecumseh Sherman was born in Lancaster, Ohio. His father, a judge of the Ohio Supreme Court, died in 1829 and left his widow with eleven children to care for. When Mrs. Sherman was forced to send some of the children to foster homes, Tecumseh, a boy of nine, was given a home by Thomas Ewing. Sherman later said, "Of all the great men amongst whom my early days were cast, the noblest Roman of them all was Thomas Ewing. A better, nobler, more intellectual man never lived."

When Mrs. Ewing had young Sherman baptized, the priest was shocked that he had the name of the famous old Indian warrior, Tecumseh. The priest added William to his name.

The military campaigns of Sherman in his March to the Sea and Marching through Georgia in the Civil War are among the famous war operations of all time. After the war, his grateful wartime comrade, General Grant, then president, made Sherman the commanding general of the army in 1869, and he held the post until 1883. He refused the Republican nomination for president in 1884 and died in New York in 1891.

Somerset, Ohio, was the home of Philip H. Sheridan. During the Civil War, General Grant hoped to find someone who could lure the attention of the public away from the daring Confederate cavalry leader, General Jeb Stuart. Sheridan proved to be right for the job. His brilliant campaign in the Shenandoah Valley was of great importance in winning the war.

Altogether, Ohio contributed the amazing total of fifty-one commanding generals in the Civil War alone.

Not a general but one of the most famous of all Ohio war heroes is the great pilot Eddie Rickenbacker, America's leading Ace of World War I, who shot down 26 German planes and earned the title of Ace of Aces. Rickenbacker was born and grew up in Columbus and had always been interested in automobiles and auto racing. Later, during World War II, Rickenbacker was forced to endure 23 days on an open rubber life raft in the Pacific after his plane made a forced landing. His book, *Seven Came Through,* is a famous account of that dreadful experience.

WRITERS AND COMPOSERS

Ohio has only one state memorial to a musician. This is the memorial to Benjamin R. Hanby, at Westerville. Benjamin Hanby was born at Rushville, Ohio, in 1833. While he was studying for the ministry, Hanby became interested in the slaves who came through his father's "station" on the Underground Railroad. One of these was Joseph Selby, who died trying to reach Canada where he hoped to earn enough money to purchase freedom for his sweetheart.

Mr. Hanby wrote the story of Selby in the form of a song, which he called "Darling Nellie Grey." It became one of the all-time hits. A few years ago it was listed as one of the eight songs whose popularity has lived through several generations.

"Darling Nellie Grey" played such an important part in the campaign against slavery that it has been called "the Uncle Tom's Cabin of song."

Sixty-eight songs were composed by Mr. Hanby. Many of these were popular in their day. Two more of his songs, "Up on the House Top" and his Christmas hymn, "Who Is He in Yonder Stall?" are still well known. The Hanby home has been restored and contains many remembrances of the Hanby family, including a large collection of the Hanby songs.

A second prominent Ohio song writer and conductor composed

A U.S. postage stamp honoring poet Paul Laurence Dunbar.

Paul Laurence
Dunbar

American poet

10 cents U.S. postage

such hit songs as "On the Road to Mandalay," "When the Boys Come Home," and "Sylvia." This was Oley Speaks, who was born in the village of Canal Winchester.

The famous song of the South, "Dixie," was not composed by a Southerner but by an Ohio man, Daniel Emmett of Mt. Vernon.

The most famous of Ohio's poets was the young Paul Laurence Dunbar, of Dayton. He was born in 1872 and grew up in poverty. His mother took in washing to keep the family alive, but she gave Paul a love of poetry and all the encouragement possible. At old Central High School in Dayton, where he was the only black, Paul Dunbar received much help on the road to being a writer.

70

To earn a living he took a job as an elevator operator in the Callahan Building, but his reputation as a poet was growing. Dodd, Mead and Company published his *Lyrics of Lonely Life,* and his friends helped him to go to England where he was given great attention.

Dunbar literally worked himself to death at the age of 34. He had published seven volumes of poetry, two volumes of short stories, and two novels. He could not seem to stop work even to try to cure the tuberculosis which finally caused his death.

For almost 30 years after her son died, his mother kept the home he had bought in Dayton and the many personal belongings of her famous son. The home and those remembrances are now preserved as a state memorial.

For almost seventy years one name was found in possibly more American homes than any other. That was the name of William H. McGuffey. The McGuffey readers, which Dr. McGuffey wrote, were used by almost every school. Seventy million McGuffey readers were sold, and several generations of American children grew up with them. They can still be bought today.

Dr. McGuffey taught at both Miami University and Cincinnati College. The great trees at Miami University have been known to generations of students as the "McGuffey elms." Dr. McGuffey was later the president of Ohio University at Athens.

Another prominent Ohio writer was the novelist William Dean Howells, ranked as one of the great men of American literature.

The "purple sage" of the far West is a long way from Zanesville, Ohio, but Zane Grey, who was born there in 1872, probably did more to make the old West popular than any other one man. Grey was a direct descendant of Ebenezer Zane, who founded Zanesville, where the future writer spent his early years and gained his love of the outdoors.

Zane Grey was a top athlete who almost made a career in professional baseball, but gave up baseball to become a dentist. After a try at dentistry, Grey became a writer, although not a very successful one until he moved to the West. There his experiences led him to write *Heritage of the Desert,* his first successful novel. *Riders of the*

Purple Sage sold the then unheard of number of two million copies, and Zane Grey's reputation was made.

Grey's writings set the pattern for almost all of the stories about the West that have followed, including the movies and TV Westerns of today. His heroes were hard-bitten and determined, of extremely moral character, always on the side of the law and justice. His villains were bad men, and his women were courageous and good.

When Zane Grey died in 1939, both he and his books had become a tradition of frontier days and a milestone in American writing.

SUCH INTERESTING PEOPLE

Many other prominent and widely different people have called Ohio home at one time or another in their lives. John D. Rockefeller gained much of his great wealth there. Bob Hope, the comedian, spent many of his early years in Cleveland and considered it his second home. Ted Lewis and the famous sharpshooter, Annie Oakley, were both Ohioans.

One unusual Ohioan whose name is a legend in America was John Chapman. Early settlers in Ohio often were surprised to find clusters of apple trees growing in unexpected places. Often these trees added a great deal to the comfort and well-being of the people. It was hard to believe that such orchards had been planted, for whoever would do such a thing would expect to make something from it, but this could not possibly be the case. Nevertheless, the trees had been planted with care by John Chapman, better known as Johnny Appleseed.

Johnny Appleseed wandered through the Ohio Valley planting his precious apple seeds. Later, he always seemed to remember where he had planted the seeds and would come back to tend and cultivate the young trees, never expecting any kind of reward except the hope that the trees would help to feed some deserving family. He spent a great deal of his time around Mansfield, Ohio. He died in 1845, and the children of Ashland have erected a memorial to this unique man.

Possibly the only one of its kind is another memorial at Carrollton,

Johnny Appleseed planted apple seeds as he wandered throughout the Ohio Valley. Besides being useful, these trees provided Ohio with beauty. Many trees have been planted in Fountain Square in Cincinnati, also.

A monument to John Chapman (Johnny Appleseed).

Ohio. This is the historic house of Major Daniel McCook, preserved in memory of the "Fighting McCooks."

Daniel McCook and his brother John had both made their home at Carrollton, where both were prominent in local activities. When the Civil War came, Daniel and his eight living sons and the five sons of John offered their services to the Union. All fourteen took an active part in the war. They became known as the "Tribe of Dan" and the "Tribe of John." From the Tribe of John there came a major general, a brigadier general, two lieutenants, a chaplain, and a navy lieutenant.

The Tribe of Dan produced three major generals, two brigadier generals, one colonel, two majors, and a private. Daniel McCook and three of his sons died in the war. The story of the Fighting McCooks is certainly one of the most extraordinary in the history of war.

Teaching and Learning

When a college or university is accepted by a recognized organization as meeting certain standards, it is said to be "accredited." At one time Ohio claimed more accredited colleges and universities than any other state. Altogether there are more than 55 schools of higher education in Ohio.

Ohio University at Athens, founded in 1809, was the first institution of higher learning in Ohio. Its Cutler Hall was the first college building in the whole Northwest Territory.

Oberlin College, at Oberlin, Ohio, was founded in 1833. Four years later there was great excitement among the students. Some were very angry with the college, while others may have been pleased although they might not have admitted it. What was the occasion for the excitement? The college had just announced that it would accept women students. Such an announcement would not attract much attention today, but at that time there were no regularly enrolled women students in U.S. colleges. Oberlin became the first coeducational college in the country. Three women graduated from Oberlin in 1841.

The music school at Oberlin is known throughout the world and is generally considered to be one of the best anywhere.

When Charles Martin Hall died, he left one third of his great estate to Oberlin College. Mr. Hall's fortune had come to him through his work in developing the aluminum industry.

Ohio State University, generally a Big Ten leader in football and other athletics, was founded in 1878. The state system now includes other universities and several community universities and colleges.

One of the reasons for the fame of Antioch College at Yellow Springs is that Horace Mann was its first president after its founding in 1853. Dr. Mann is considered to be one of the greatest men in the history of education.

The famous Western Reserve University at Cleveland recalls the early history of the area when Connecticut kept title to lands in Ohio and called these her "Western Reserve."

Children tour the central kitchen of Dayton where over 20,000 school lunches are packaged daily.

Hiram College, Kenyon College, and Mt. Union College are other prominent Ohio schools. Mt. Union introduced the first summer school held anywhere. Case Institute of Technology, at Cleveland, was the first college of technology west of the Alleghenies.

Enchantment of Ohio

ENCHANTED TRACES OF VANISHED PEOPLES

The things they left behind tell us all we know about many of the prehistoric people who called Ohio their home. Some of the most interesting remains of early civilizations are still to be seen in Ohio, and most of these have been carefully preserved and cared for by the state.

A "snake" more than a quarter of a mile (.4 kilometer) long lies coiled along the bank of a creek near the village of Loudon. From the air it seems to be a long ridge of dirt twisted into seven great curves, with its tail coiled up. This enormous "reptile" is swallowing something which seems to be an egg. It has been called the finest serpent effigy in the U.S. These "effigies" were made by early people, in the form of turtles, birds, serpents, and other animals.

No one knows which one of Ohio's prehistoric peoples made this giant figure or why. After digging in it to try and unearth burial places, the experts decided it was a solid ridge of soil without graves or anything else placed inside. Apparently the builders planned the design carefully since flat stones and lumps of clay were laid on the original ground surface as a guide plan. Then baskets of earth were brought and carefully emptied in place. Without any earth-moving machines or trucks, this work must have taken the labor of hundreds of people over a long time. Since 1900 the entire serpent mound region has been operated as a state memorial.

On the top of a hill in Highland County, visitors can see another of Ohio's unusual tourist attractions. This is a fort built by prehistoric Indians. Again, no one is sure which one of the Indian groups carried all the earth up the slope in baskets to build the great wall that runs for more than half a mile. The height of the wall varies from 6 to 15 feet (1.8 to 4.5 meters), and it is about 40 feet (12 meters) through at the base. It encloses an area of 40 acres (16 hectares). There are 33 openings in the wall, and it is thought that there may have been wooden gates in each of these.

Those who view this ancient fort may well wonder what great need caused these people to struggle to build such an enormous earthworks.

An even larger "fort" built in much the same way is preserved as Fort Ancient State Memorial near Lebanon. The walls of this fort are 3½ miles (6 kilometers) long and enclose 100 acres (40 hectares). The pottery, tools, implements, and ornaments found in and around the fort indicate that it was built by the Hopewell Indians.

Within the walls of the fort are burial mounds and indications that the inner part of the fort was used for living purposes. After the Hopewell Indians had disappeared, another group of prehistoric Indians occupied the fort, and these are called the Fort Ancient Indians.

They may have lived there as late as 1650, after Europeans had already made a number of settlements on the East Coast, but no record has been found that Europeans ever saw the Fort Ancient Indians or that the Fort Ancient Indians ever saw the Hopewell Indians who originally built Fort Ancient.

Still another series of Hopewell mounds is preserved as a state memorial at Newark. A part of this is the famous Eagle Effigy, built up in the shape of an eagle.

At least one Ohio town actually takes its name from the works of the mound builders. The village of Circleville was laid out in the form of the circular mounds on its site, and it was given its name because of this interesting pattern.

RELIVING THE ENCHANTMENT OF THE PIONEERS

"Adena—a name given to places remarkable for the delightfulness of their situations." That was the Hebrew meaning for the name which Thomas Worthington gave his beautiful estate at Chillicothe. It was there that the preparations were made for Ohio to become a state. In fact, Worthington has been called "the father of Ohio statehood." He served for two terms in the U.S. Senate from Ohio and also was governor for two terms.

Restored as Adena State Memorial, the estate appears to visitors

Overlooking Cincinnati from the top of the Hilton Hotel.

today as one of the best examples of the gracious living men and women of good taste and wealth could have even in such early days in pioneer settlements.

In memory of the first settlement in Ohio and of those brave first settlers, the state has built a museum on the site of the fort built to protect that first settlement at Marietta. The fort was called Campus Martius. It was considered to be a grand structure.

Museum visitors there can see one of the finest collections of items used by pioneer families. Also near the museum the Sons and Daughters of Pioneer Rivermen have established a River Museum.

For many years Marietta was a busy center for building ships. The prosperity of Marietta and all the other river towns depended mainly on the shipment of merchandise by boat. Only ten years after the first steamboat puffed down the Ohio River from Pittsburgh to Cincinnati in 1811, 75 steamboats were operating on the river. Thirty years later there were 450.

Many boats had elegant barrooms and card rooms. Their passengers danced to orchestra music. Beside the colorful passenger boats, there were floating libraries and stores and glamorous showboats.

But the glamorous, puffing old steamboat with its churning paddlewheels disappeared from the river. Today's diesel is more efficient. Now, twice as much freight moves up and down the Ohio River system as passes through the Panama Canal.

One of the old steam stern-wheelers, named the *W.P. Snyder, Jr.,* was donated to the River Museum at Marietta by the Crucible Steel Company. Today, visitors to the museum can see the kind of boat that first brought greatness to the Ohio Valley.

The memory of Ohio's pioneer life is kept throughout the state. Near New Philadelphia, the Schoenbrunn Village, where the Moravian Indian converts were massacred, has been restored. The meeting house of the Quakers, or Friends as they call themselves, near Mt. Pleasant, has been restored and visitors may still see the large brick meeting place as it looked when it was first built in 1814.

RELIVING WARTIME PERIL

In peace, the memories of Ohio's wartime sacrifice are still preserved, although most of the original buildings have disappeared, torn down to make way for progress.

Old Fort Washington, which protected the early settlers at Cincinnati, has not been preserved. In fact, its exact location had been lost somewhere among the paved streets and tall modern buildings of the city, although the old plans of the fort are still in existence. One day, in digging the basement for a new building, the excavators uncovered the powder magazine of the old fort, almost intact. Now it is possible to trace the outline of Fort Washington, and a bronze marker on an insurance building shows where the old powder magazine was discovered.

The war whoops have died away; almost two hundred years have passed, and yet visitors to Fort Recovery still have a feeling of being present where great events took place. A tall monument and a rebuilt part of the old fort remind the sightseers of the awful defeat of Governor St. Clair which took place here, of "Mad" Anthony Wayne, who built a fort on the spot and called it Fort Recovery because he hoped it would "recover" the victory, and who held off the largest army of Indians ever gathered together. This is a quiet town that still recalls its memories.

A tall monument and some graves of war heroes are all that remain at Perrysburg to remind visitors of the events that took place there when Fort Meigs, which William Henry Harrison had built, was attacked by the British. Before the attack, the Americans had dug bomb-proof trenches, where they were forced to sleep and eat for several days. For four days, the British hurled cannon balls at the fort and its defenders. Then reinforcements came for Fort Meigs. A truce was arranged for burial and exchange of prisoners. Today these sunken and grass-grown graves of the fallen soldiers can still be seen. The British came back to the attack, but Fort Meigs was stronger than ever and after nine days the British retreated to Canada.

A granite shaft, the tallest Doric column in the world, rising 352 feet (107 meters) above the waters of Lake Erie, is a constant reminder of one of America's great naval victories. This is the Perry Memorial near Sandusky. Nine states and the federal government combined to build this massive monument on South Bass Island of Put-in-Bay, which was finished in 1915. Above the observation platform is a penthouse with navigation lights, and still higher a lighted bronze urn. Beneath the rotunda three American and three British officers are buried.

Memories of the Civil War are recalled by visits to the house where General U.S. Grant was born at Point Pleasant, and General William T. Sherman's birthplace at Lancaster. When plans were made to tear down the Sherman House and replace it with an apartment building, the community of Lancaster purchased the property and donated it to the state as a memorial to Lancaster's most famous son.

ENCHANTMENT OF CLEVELAND

Cleveland was founded in 1796 by Moses Cleaveland. No one is quite sure how the spelling of the name was changed, but the story is that a newspaperman left out the extra "a" in the name because it was too long to fit in a column he was writing. However it happened, Mr. Cleaveland's city has been Cleveland almost since the beginning.

The site where Moses Cleaveland founded Cleveland.

A dramatic view of Cleveland from Lake Erie.

Sixteen years after it was founded there were still only about 60 people in Cleveland. But today it is the largest city in Ohio and one of the great cities of America. The city grew slowly as a trading center. The coming of the canal from Cleveland to Portsmouth and the growing traffic on Lake Erie brought the city steady growth.

With the expansion of such activities as John D. Rockefeller's Standard Oil Company, Cleveland began to grow rapidly, overtook Cincinnati and continues to grow and expand today. The city's vast improvement program is adding almost $2,000,000,000 to the metropolitan redevelopment. The city-county Justice Center occupies an entire block in the heart of the city and was completed in 1976.

Visitors today find an interesting and bustling city. Public Square is the heart of Cleveland. Soldiers and Sailors Monument in the center of the square honors veterans of the Civil War. Rising above Public Square is the 52-story Terminal Towers, at one time the tallest building in the United States ouside of New York. Cleveland has one of the finest symphony orchestras anywhere, and her art museum presents one of the great collections of art.

The first museum of its kind in the country was Cleveland Health Museum. This popular museum helps to impress on people the importance of health. Visitors straighten their shoulders as they pass the posture charts, and all move the levers on the calorie charts to see how many calories are in their favorite desserts.

The most unusual of Cleveland's many parks is Rockefeller Park, with its Cultural Gardens, which have no duplicate anywhere else.

83

ENCHANTMENT OF COLUMBUS

The gray limestone capitol building is one of the most interesting places to visit in Columbus. In the center of the inlaid marble floor beneath the great dome of the building are blocks of marble, each representing one of the original 13 states. Outside the blocks, there are circles of marble, standing for the territory of Ohio before it was organized, the Louisiana Purchase, and the land acquired by the United States from the Mexican War. Outside the last circle is a sunburst of 32 points, one for each state when the floor was laid.

Although this capitol building has a modern look because of its simple lines, its cornerstone was placed in 1839. But the capitol took 22 years to finish, so that it was not really completed until 1861, the year the Civil War began. Before it was finally complete, five different architects had served under 12 different governors. The contractor vowed he would not put up a "temporary" building. With foundation walls 11 to 15 feet (3 to 5 meters) thick, Ohio's capitol building was built to last.

The state capitol building in Columbus.

Ice fishing

One of Ohio's most interesting monuments is found on the northwest corner of the capitol grounds. This is the statue called "Ohio's Jewels," which was made for the World's Fair in Chicago in 1893. When the fair was over, the people of Ohio took up a fund to move it back to their state. It takes its name from the Roman mother, Cornelia, who had no precious stones for jewels but she called her children her "jewels." Levi Tucker Scofield, the sculptor, placed a statue of Cornelia at the top of a pedestal. Around the base he put his selection of Ohio's jewels—statues of Grant, Sherman, Sheridan, Stanton, Garfield, Hayes, and Chase.

Columbus is also the home of one of the great state fairs. Among the interesting exhibits on the Ohio State Fair Grounds is a reproduction of William Henry Harrison's house.

The Pro Football Hall of Fame in Canton, showing Jim Thorpe's statue.

OTHER ENCHANTMENT HIGHLIGHTS

A model of the "House That Jack Built" may be seen at Bellaire, Ohio. This may not seem unusual at first, but Jack was a little mule. He helped his master, Jake Heatherington, make his mining fortune. When Heatherington retired, he built a fine house and lived there with his little mule until both died.

Kelley's Island in Lake Erie, near Sandusky, is famous for the grooves and marks cut into the rock by the glaciers. This area has been called "one of the best examples of glacial action in the world." The story of what happened as the glaciers moved back and forth for millions of years has been cut right into the rock, and archeologists can read this "record" almost as easily as a book. Also on Kelley's Island is Inscription Rock, a boulder on which prehistoric men carved their symbols.

The largest U.S. Air Force research field is Wright-Patterson, on the site near Dayton where earlier the Wright Brothers had tested their theories and where they flew after their first flight at Kitty Hawk, NC. Also at Wright-Patterson Field is a fine national aeronautics museum.

For anyone interested in the outdoors and conservation of our natural resources, the Muskingum Watershed Conservancy District will be especially interesting. This is the group of dams and other projects built in the watershed of the Muskingum River to keep the water from running downstream so fast and, in that way, to help control the awful floods that used to sweep down the river.

Ohio was a pioneer in this kind of work. The first such conservancy district in the nation was the Miami District. The successful activities of conservancy districts have been studied all over the world. They are among the first and best examples of what is called complete watershed conservation.

One of the world's famous bridges is also on the Muskingum River, at Zanesville. This is one of the few bridges shaped in the form of a "Y"—a bridge that actually has three ends.

Hocking State Park is one of Ohio's dozens of interesting recreational state parks. At Hocking the visitor sees a rock canyon wilderness as awesome as many in the West, especially surprising in an area so close to so many cities and large towns. In addition to the state parks, Ohio has about 60 historical parks or memorials and more than 300 roadside parks.

Each year a hill in Akron is the scene of one of the world's unique races. Thousands of people line the specially built track at Derby Downs. This sloping asphalt strip is used only for Akron's famous Soap Box Derby. Boys from all over the country race down the slope in their motorless cars for prizes worth thousands of dollars in scholarships.

However, for those who visit or live in Ohio, the state itself is "prize" enough.

Handy Reference Section

Instant Facts

Became 17th state—March 1, 1803
Nickname—The Buckeye State
State motto—With God, All Things Are Possible
State bird—Cardinal
State insect—Ladybug
State tree—Buckeye
State flower—Scarlet carnation
State stone—Ohio flint
State beverage—Tomato juice
State song—"Beautiful Ohio"
Area—41,222 square miles (106,764 square kilometers)
Rank in area—35th
Greatest length (north to south)—210 miles (338 kilometers)
Greatest width (east to west)—230 miles (370 kilometers)
Geographic center—25 miles (40 kilometers) north northeast of Columbus
Highest point—1,550 feet (472 meters), Campbell Hill
Lowest point—433 feet (132 meters), Ohio River
Mean elevation—850 feet (259 meters)
Number of counties—88
Population—10,797,624 (1980 census)
Rank in population—6th
Population density—261 persons per square mile (101 persons per square kilometer) 1980 census
Rank in density—9th
Population center—In Morrow County, 7.8 miles (12.5 kilometers) east of New Gilead
Illiteracy rate—0.8 percent
Birthrate—15 per 1,000
Physicians per 100,000—137

Principal cities—		
Cleveland	573,822	(1980 census)
Columbus	565,032	
Cincinnati	385,457	
Toledo	354,635	
Akron	237,177	
Dayton	193,536	

You Have a Date with History

1670—Explorations of La Salle
1748—Ohio Company of Virginia organized to settle Ohio
1750—Exploration of Christopher Gist
1763—Britain takes control from France
1764—Indians return prisoners at Coshocton
1774—Treaty ends Lord Dunmore's War
1787—Northwest Territory established
1788—First permanent settlement in Ohio, at Marietta
1788—Cincinnati founded
1791—St. Clair defeated by Little Turtle
1793—First newspaper published
1795—Treaty of Green Ville ended Indian wars
1796—Cleveland founded
1800—Ohio made a separate territory
1803—Ohio admitted as a state
1804—Ohio steel industry begins
1811—First steamboat on Ohio River
1813—Perry's victory at Put-in-Bay
1816—Capital moved to Columbus from Chillicothe
1836—Boundary dispute with Michigan settled
1840—William Henry Harrison elected president
1848—First successful railroad
1861—Civil War
1868—Ulysses S. Grant elected president
1870—Standard Oil Company founded
1877—Rutherford B. Hayes becomes president
1880—James A. Garfield elected president
1896—William McKinley elected president
1901—Adena prehistoric people recognized
1908—William Howard Taft elected president
1913—Flood of 1913
1920—Warren Gamaliel Harding elected president
1937—Flood of 1937
1952—Portsmouth atomic project opened
1955—Ohio Turnpike opened
1959—St. Lawrence Seaway opened
1963—State begins giant economic development program
1969—Neil Armstrong becomes first human being to step on the moon
1971—Ohio adopts an income tax
1974—John Glenn wins Senate seat
1977—Howard Metzenbaum regains Senate seat at expense of Robert Taft, Jr.
1979—Ohio agrees to pay $675,000 to families of dead and injured in Kent State
      shootings
1985—Multiple tornadoes rampage in Ohio leaving 6 dead, 240 injured, and
      enormous property damage

Thinkers, Doers, Fighters

Men and Women Who Helped Make Ohio Great

Charles F. Brush
John Chapman
Moses Cleaveland
Manasseh Cutler
Paul Laurence Dunbar
James A. Garfield
Benjamin Franklin Goodrich
Ulysses Simpson Grant
Zane Grey
Charles Martin Hall
Warren Gamaliel Harding
Benjamin Harrison
William Henry Harrison
Rutherford B. Hayes
Herbert W. Hoover
Charles F. Kettering
William H. McGuffey
William McKinley
Rufus Putnam

John Rankin
Eddie Rickenbacker
James Ritty
Arthur St. Clair
Philip H. Sheridan
William Tecumseh Sherman
Oley Speaks
Benjamin Stites
Harriet Beecher Stowe
Charles Phelps Taft
Robert A. Taft
William Howard Taft
Chief Tarhe
Edward Tiffin
Lew Wallace
Anthony Wayne
Thomas Worthington
Orville Wright
Wilbur Wright

Governors of Ohio

Edward Tiffin 1803-1807
Thomas Kirker 1807-1808
Samuel Huntington 1808-1810
Return Jonathan Meigs 1810-1814
Othneil Looker 1814
Thomas Worthington 1814-1818
Ethan Allen Brown 1818-1822
Allen Trimble 1822 and 1826-1830
Jeremiah Morrow 1822-1826
Duncan McArthur 1830-1832
Robert Lucas 1832-1836
Joseph Vance 1836-1838
Wilson Shannon 1838-1840 and
    1842-1844
Thomas Corwin 1840-1842
Thomas W. Bartley 1844
Mordecai Bartley 1844-1846
William Bebb 1846-1848
Seabury Ford 1848-1850
Reuben Wood 1850-1853
William Medill 1853-1856
Salmon P. Chase 1856-1860
William Dennison Jr. 1860-1862
David Tod 1862-1864
John Brough 1864-1865
Charles Anderson 1865-1866
Jacob Dolson Cox 1866-1868
Rutherford B. Hayes 1868-1872 and
    1876-1877
Edward F. Noyes 1872-1874
William Allen 1874-1876

Thomas L. Young 1877-1878
Richard M. Bishop 1878-1880
Charles Foster 1880-1884
George Hoadly 1884-1886
Joseph B. Foraker 1886-1890
James E. Campbell 1890-1892
William McKinley 1892-1896
Asa S. Bushnell 1896-1900
George K. Nash 1900-1904
Myron T. Herrick 1904-1906
John M. Pattison 1906
Andrew L. Harris 1906-1909
Judson Harmon 1909-1913
James M. Cox 1913-1915 and
    1917-1921
Frank B. Willis 1915-1917
Harry L. Davis 1921-1923
Vic Donahey 1923-1929
Myers Y. Cooper 1929-1931
George White 1931-1935
Martin L. Davey 1935-1939
John W. Bricker 1939-1945
Frank J. Lausche 1945-1947 and
    1949-1957
Thomas J. Herbert 1947-1949
John W. Brown 1957
C. William O'Neill 1957-1959
Michael V. DiSalle 1959-1963
James A. Rhodes 1963-1971
John J. Gilligan 1971-1975
James A. Rhodes 1975-1983
Richard Celeste 1983-

Index

93

PICTURE CREDITS

ABOUT THE AUTHOR

With the publication of his first book for school use when he was twenty, **Allan Carpenter** began a career as an author that has spanned more than 135 books. After teaching in the public schools of Des Moines, Mr. Carpenter began his career as an educational publisher at the age of twenty-one when he founded the magazine *Teachers Digest*. In the field of educational periodicals, he was responsible for many innovations. During his many years in publishing, he has perfected a highly organized approach to handling large volumes of factual material: after extensive traveling and having collected all possible materials, he systematically reviews and organizes everything. From his apartment high in Chicago's John Hancock Building, Allan recalls, "My collection and assimilation of materials on the states and countries began before the publication of my first book." Allan is the founder of Carpenter Publishing House and of Infordata International, Inc., publishers of *Issues in Education* and *Index to U. S. Government Periodicals*. When he is not writing or traveling, his principal avocation is music. He has been the principal bassist of many symphonies, and he managed the country's leading non-professional symphony for twenty-five years.

96